SPY 101
INTRO TO ESPIONAGE

BY TREY "SUPER SPY" KING

SCHOLASTIC

Copyright © 2014 by Scholastic Inc. All rights reserved.
Published by Scholastic Inc. SCHOLASTIC and associated logos are trademarks and/or registered trademarks of Scholastic Inc.

ISBN 978-0-545-73137-9

12 11 10 9 8   15 16 17 18 19/0

Printed in the U.S.A.   40
First printing, September 2014
Illustrated by C.S. Jennings
Designed by Rocco Melillo

Photos ©: Cover red button and throughout: Viktorus/Shutterstock, Inc.; cover borders and title background: Mur34/Shutterstock, Inc.; cover bottom green keypad: szsz/Shutterstock, Inc.; cover top left purple screen: snapgalleria/Shutterstock, Inc.; cover slider bars and throughout: YasnaTen/Shutterstock, Inc.; cover monitors: osov/Shutterstock, Inc.; cover gauges: Natykach Nataliia/Shutterstock, Inc.; 1 monitor: osov/Shutterstock, Inc.; 2 icons and throughout: Pongsuwan/ Shutterstock, Inc.; 4 background: pixelparticle/Shutterstock, Inc.; 6 top button and throughout: rvrspb/Shutterstock, Inc.; 7 bottom left: Shpak Anton/Shutterstock, Inc.; 12 bottom left: Maxim Maksutov/Shutterstock, Inc.; 13: Mat Hayward/ Shutterstock, Inc.; 14 bottom left: Bachrach/Archive Photos/Getty Images; 15 top right: Sporting News via Getty Images; 15 bottom right: Columbia Pictures/Photofest; 20 bottom left: De Agostini Picture Library/ Getty Images; 21 bottom right: Hulton Archive/Getty Images; 21 top right: AP Images; 27: Sergey Mironov/ Shutterstock, Inc.; 30 bottom right: Popperfoto/Getty Images; 30-31 button lights and dashes: Pixachi/Shutterstock, Inc.; 31 top: Gamma-Rapho via Getty Images; 31 center: Hulton Archive/Getty Images; 31 bottom: Time & Life Pictures/Getty Images; 36 wavelength: Mack7777/Shutterstock, Inc.

Psssssttt. Hey, you!

Yes, YOU. What are you doing here? You shouldn't be reading this. You don't have the clearance. What's that? Oh, you're one of the trainees, huh? Well, I guess I'll allow you to read this book . . .

Welcome to Spy 101. Do you think you're ready to enter the secret underworld of espionage? It won't be easy, but I can teach you the basics. You ready? What you mean you have to go to the bathroom? Spies go to the bathroom! Oh, wait . . . yeah, they do. Er go, too.

BE RIGHT BACK.

TABLE OF CONTENTS

MISSION GUIDE!

WHAT'S A SPY?

YEAH, SURE, YOU THINK
YOU KNOW WHAT A SPY IS,
BUT DO YOU REALLY KNOW
WHAT A SPY IS?

It's a person who gathers intelligence. Kind of like a student at school, learning all he can about subjects like math and science—except it's a lot more dangerous when you're a spy.

Why? Because you are gathering "intel" (a fancy way of saying information) from a person or group that doesn't want you to know what they know. Like how your parents don't want you to know the truth about swallowing gum (. . . it does not take seven years to digest), or your teacher doesn't want you to know the answers to your history pop quiz tomorrow (the answer is "1492").

The art or practice of spying is sometimes called espionage by governments, businesses, and adults with good vocabularies. Now, in most cases, it is quite illegal and you can make some people really mad by nosing into their affairs. So make sure that if you're going to spy, you choose your target carefully. If you get in trouble, then I get in trouble, and if I get in trouble, I'm going to be really upset, and then I won't tell you any more of my awesome secrets...

Who am I **kidding?**
I'll tell you **everything**
I know.

TOP SECRET

HOW LONG HAVE SPIES BEEN AROUND?

PRETTY MUCH SINCE THE DAWN OF MANKIND!

You think I'm kidding, but I'm not. As long as there have been organized people and tribes, there have also been spies. Ancient Chinese and Indian military folk used deception and subversion tactics to learn about their enemies. In ancient Egypt, the pharaohs developed entire spy networks. Even the ancient Aztecs, Hebrews, Greeks, Romans, and Mongols had spies. Of course, I think some of the coolest early spies belonged to feudal Japan—they had ninjas gather intelligence!

In more recent times, spies have become a popular sensation in books, TV, and even movies. Famous writers like Rudyard Kipling and James Fenimore Cooper wrote about spies over a hundred years ago, though it was probably Ian Fleming's James Bond series that garnered the most fame. Agent 007 was the hero of twelve novels, two short story collections, and dozens of hit movies.

More About Ninjas

Feudal Japan was considered the medieval period in Japanese history. In European medieval times, they had knights and kings and maidens and dragons. (Dragons are real, right?) But in Japan, they had powerful families (the daimyo), military warlords (the shogun), and yes, ninjas!

A ninja (also known as shinobi) was a secret agent or mercenary in feudal Japan. Their tasks included everything from espionage and infiltration to sabotage and assassination. They were sneaky about everything they did and tried to stick to the shadows and nighttime whenever possible. They weren't very nice guys and were pretty much the opposite of the esteemed samurai—members of the military nobility who observed very strict rules about honor and combat. While a ninja wouldn't hesitate to stab you in the back, a samurai would insist you face him in honorable combat, even if it meant his death.

Over the years, stories about ninjas have become somewhat legendary, especially in popular culture. Movies and books often mix historical fact with myth, showing the shinobi as having mysterious powers—like invisibility, walking on water, and control over elements like fire and wind. Yes, perhaps they were mystical warriors, but they started out as spies. What would you rather be?

Hi-YAH!

Hi-YAH!

WHAT'S YOUR ALIAS?

AN ALIAS, OR A "HANDLE,"
IS A SECRET CODE NAME.

If I were a spy—which I totally am—then my handle would be something like "Sneaky Phoenix." Why? A phoenix is a bird that bursts into flames and is reborn from its own ashes, which I think is pretty neat. (Plus it was in Harry Potter, one of my favorite book series.)

So what would your handle be? Animal names are always cool (like The Hawk or Wolverine or King Panda). So are names from history or myths (like George Washington or Poseidon). It can be something mysterious (like Mr. Shadow), or something that inspires both fear and awe (like The Ghost). Or it can be something weird (like The Invisible Chair), or maybe something that describes you (like Shorty). Or you can just pick something that sounds really daring and awesome (like The Crimson Hood or Batman). Waita minute! I think Batman is already taken . . .

Need help? Here's a list of cool adjectives and nouns. Pick one from each column or mix and match. Write your own ideas at the bottom.

Doctor Tiger

Dark	Saber
Hidden	Tiger
Slippery	Dragon
Scarlet	Hulk
Violent	Beast
Rampaging	Avenger
Dangerous	Eel
Quiet	Lightning
Black	Muscle
Silver	Fox
Professional	Midnight
Doctor	Creep

SQUIB!

SLIP!

Slippery Fox

WHY DO YOU NEED A CODE NAME?

TO *PROTECT* YOUR LOVED ONES...
OF COURSE!

Just like Superman's secret identity is mild-mannered news reporter Clark Kent, you need to protect your normal self from your super-spy self. If you sign your secret transmissions with your name, phone number, and email address, it'll be really easy for your enemies to attack. Then they can find you, destroy your house with a giant laser cannon, send cyborg gorillas to attack you, and then kidnap your parents and feed them to tigers. Yes, you might think that'd be funny, but later you'll come to regret it since your parents give you money for stuff like ice cream.

It's always good to have a secret operative name—that way, when you communicate with other spies, you can do so by secret means. For hundreds of years, secret agents have used code names to throw other spies and rival governments off their trail. The best way to keep an air of mystery and intrigue about yourself is to not be yourself—be someone else. Once you have a code name in place, then even if your secret communications are found, the enemy won't know who you are. They'll be all, "Who is General Catfish?" and they'll have no way to trace it back to you. Ha! Better luck next time, villain!

TRUE SPY STORIES!

SPIES ON THE SIDE!

Some spies have day jobs—like being famous. Whe[ ] an actor, a writer, or a baseball player, these [ ] prove you can have two careers at the same ti[ ] even if one of those jobs is being a secret spy!

 ## Julia Child

Julia Child may be known the world over as a famous chef, but before she began cooking, she was a researcher for the Office of Strategic Service (OSS) during World War II, the forerunner of today's Central Intelligence Agency (also known as the CIA).

Moe Berg

Boston Red Sox catcher Moe Berg traveled to Japan in 1934 on a baseball all-star tour with Babe Ruth and Lou Gehrig. What his fans didn't know was that he spoke seven languages, snuck confidential films across borders, evaluated atomic research, and served in the Secret Intelligence Branch for the OSS.

Sterling Hayden

American actor Sterling Hayden was known for his roles in Westerns and film noir movies, but he secretly ran weapons to partisans fighting Nazis and parachuted into Fascist-controlled Croatia. Later, he was awarded the Silver Star for his undercover work during World War II.

TOOLS OF THE TRADE

NO MATTER WHAT YOUR JOB IS,
YOU NEED **TOOLS.**

Carpenters need saws for their jobs, and so do doctors (though probably cleaner ones). And a spy needs tools, too. Spies have to be inconspicuous (meaning, they need to be able to blend in with a crowd), so they can't walk around with all this gear. But a good spy knows to plan ahead.

Make sure you have whatever you need before a mission. A few basics are listed below that will help in almost any scenario*:

*DEPENDING ON YOUR MISSION, OF COURSE!

Flashlight – *for dark places.*

Magnifying glass – *if you need to look for clues.*

Small notebook – *if you need to write down important details.*

Pencil and/or pen – *for writing, right?*

Camera – *a spy's best friend!*

Soft cloth or gloves – *for picking up evidence and not getting your fingerprints on the evidence.*

Fingerprint kit – *this is for the hard-core detective, but it doesn't hurt a spy to be able to pick up fingerprints.*

Swiss Army Knife – *these are good to have in general, and you never know when you're going to need one. Just make sure you don't stab your eye out!*

Compass – *unless you can read the sun and the stars, a compass is always good to have when you're tracking someone. It can help you find your directions, especially if you're using a map.*

Computer, laptop, or smart-phone – *it's amazing what you can look up on the Internet these days.*

Tape (duct or Scotch) – *there's a hundred uses for tape! Stay tuned!*

Digital audio recorder – *in case you can get up close and personal to record a confession.*

Plastic bags – *for putting evidence in.*

First-aid kit – *okay, call me crazy, but I like to be prepared for the worst. Hopefully you won't get stabbed by a ninja, but it's always good to know how to fix yourself up if you scrape your knee.*

Black clothes – *to help you hide in the shadows and look cool.*

Black hat with eyeholes – *to keep your ears warm if it's cold.*

Binoculars – *for long-distance spying!*

Walkie-talkies – *if you're working with a partner, these are great.*

Snacks – *what? I get hungry really easily. And no one likes a cranky spy!*

Backpack – *if you intend to carry some or all of this stuff, make sure you have something to put it all in!*

> **A GOOD SPY IS FIT,**
> **FROM HEAD TO TOE.**

That means he's not just physically able, but mentally keen as well. After all, a brain is a spy's most important muscle. Spies can't just be giant, muscular brutes—they have to be smarter than the average person. That means having lots of different skills and a mind that is quick to adapt to new or changing situations.

Just like in the movies, a good spy should be able to hack into a computer database, solve a hundred-year-old puzzle, or break into the Vatican in Rome! Okay, so maybe you don't have to be quite that good yet, but a good place to start is getting your mind sharp and speeding up those reflexes. Memory, attention, problem-solving, speed, and creativity are all essential to a good spy.

There are all kinds of ways to sharpen your mind.
A few suggestions are below:

Break Your Routine – This may sound weird, but something as simple as brushing your teeth with your left hand (if you're a righty) can help your brain learn a new way of thinking. Another way to break up your routine? Jog backward!

Play Games – Whether it's a crossword puzzle, a jigsaw puzzle, chess, Sudoku, or even a board game with friends, make sure to play. It helps train the mind to think of creative solutions and forces you to focus. For an extra challenge, time yourself, and then try to shorten your time each game you play.

Hydrate Your Mind – Your brain is 80 percent water, so if it isn't hydrated enough, it'll slow down. So make sure you drink plenty of water and keep those neurons firing!

Get Some Shut-Eye – Lack of sleep inhibits learning, concentration, and memory—three things essential to a good spy. So make sure to get a good night's rest if you want to have the energy to save the world.

Read, Read, Read! – I know what you're thinking—"I'm reading right now!" Well, good for you. Keep up the good work. The more you know, the better chance you have of outwitting your enemy in a mind-to-mind battle.

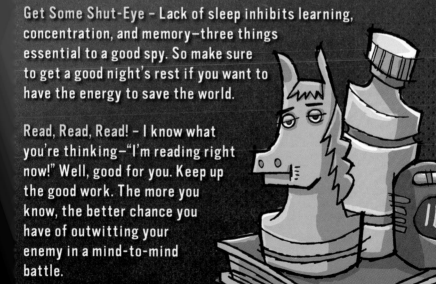

TRUE SPY STORIES!

THE *BEST SPIES* HAVE LOTS OF *TALENTS...*

A good way to practice being a spy is to be good at lots of stuff. Check out these spies with long résumés and lots of skills.

Christopher Marlowe

He isn't as well-known as his friend William Shakespeare, but Christopher Marlowe was still a man of many talents. He was an English playwright, a brilliant scholar, and a part-time amateur spy for Queen Elizabeth. In 1580, he was a student at Cambridge but was often absent. The university was going to flunk him until they received a letter from the queen saying he was working in her "Majesty's good service."

Sir William Samuel Stephenson

No list of spies would be complete without at least a mention of the man who inspired the creation of James Bond—Sir William Samuel Stephenson! Better known as "Intrepid" (a code name given him by Winston Churchill), Stephenson was a fighter pilot, a boxing champion, a businessman, an inventor, and the senior representative of British Intelligence during World War II. He also founded a secret training camp for spies in Canada called Camp X, though its graduates had a different name for it—the Ottawa School of Murder & Mayhem!

Roald Dahl

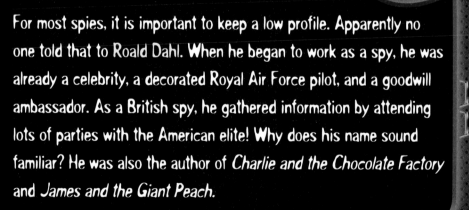

For most spies, it is important to keep a low profile. Apparently no one told that to Roald Dahl. When he began to work as a spy, he was already a celebrity, a decorated Royal Air Force pilot, and a goodwill ambassador. As a British spy, he gathered information by attending lots of parties with the American elite! Why does his name sound familiar? He was also the author of *Charlie and the Chocolate Factory* and *James and the Giant Peach.*

THE FIVE SENSES

SPY TOOLS YOU WERE BORN WITH

Now that you know most of the tools you need at your disposal to be a good spy, I should let you in on a little secret? The five most important tools you already have—seeing, hearing, smelling, tasting, and touching.

It may seem pretty basic, but if you think about it, it makes a whole lot of sense. A spy can smell poison in his beverage before he drinks it. A spy can hear the buzzing of electricity before he hops an enemy's fence. And a spy can see when someone has a giant sword and is about to—WATCH OUT! Whew, that was a close one!

The best way to hone these inherent skills is to practice them.

SEEING – Set a stopwatch and give yourself twenty seconds to memorize a sentence in a book. Do it again with a new sentence, but this time only give yourself ten seconds. Then again, but with five seconds. Keep playing until your sight memory gets sharper.

HEARING – Try the same game as the previous one, but do it with music, or with a TV show. This skill will help you to focus and concentrate, and eventually you'll be able to remember entire conversations.

TASTING – Do you like to eat? Ask your parents if you can come to dinner this week with a blindfold. Then sit down and eat and see if you can guess what the dish is and what the ingredients are. Get extra credit by having your parents add different seasonings.

TOUCHING– Have you ever played Marco Polo in the swimming pool? This is an excellent exercise for a spy. Instead of relying on your sight or even sounds, rely on the movement of the water around you. Let the movement in the water tell you where your opponents are. Not only will you be on your way to being a spy, but maybe even a Kung Fu master!

SMELLING – This sense is often overlooked, but can be invaluable if you learn to use it. Start taking note of different smells, like your teacher's perfume or your friend's favorite flavor of gum. Eventually, you'll be able to hone your olfactory palate.

SNIFF SNIFF

A GOOD SMILE GOES A LONG WAY!

Now that you are in shape, smart as a whip, a
have a cool alias, it's time to delve into the nit
gritty of being a super spy. But first, it's time for
attitude adjustment . . . it's time to talk about cha
Now, before you get sadface and say, "I couldn't
less charming if I were a snaggle-toothed old goat .
I'd like to point out that anyone can be charming.

Have you seen those chill, suave spies on 1
They walk into a room like they own the place, a
everyone turns their way to get a look at the cool a
mysterious stranger. That is certainly one way
charm others. This is an "**overt**," or open and obvio
method of spying. These spies like to make a big
trance, and draw attention to themselves. That w
they are hiding in plain sight! They engage everyo
in a room, using their charms to make others comfc
able, and then score valuable information.

Being charming is easy. Here are a few pointers:

- The first rule is easy: SMILE! Everyone appreciates a good smile and a simple "Hello, how are you?"

- Compliment the person. This is a great way to start the conversation. Once the person feels appreciated, they're more likely to talk to you.

- Ask the other person about their life. Remember, everyone likes to talk about themselves! And don't forget, be nice.

- Find a topic to discuss, and then actively listen. Don't look around the room, but instead focus directly on the person.

- When you're ready, and the person is comfortable talking to you, turn the conversation to a topic you want to know about. Then subtly get the information you need for your mission.

To practice this style of operation, have a conversation with someone you usually wouldn't. Perhaps ask a neighbor about her cat, or ask your parents about their jobs. Even if you find their story incredibly boring, act interested and ask them a lot of questions. Maybe you'll learn something useful that you didn't know before. Spies love information of all kinds. You never know when it may become useful.

WINK!

STEALTH MODE

THERE ARE ALL KINDS OF METHODS OF SPYING AND GETTING **INFORMATION**.

You just read about one where you talk to people and charm them into divulging their secrets. But another style is to get information without talking to anybody. Acting **"covertly"** is more subtle, like the spy who uses stealth and quiet to operate.

If you've watched movies or read books about spies, you'll recognize this mode of operation. This type of spy sneaks in the back door late at night, using the shadows to stay hidden. He always knows the layout of the place he's invading, and he knows how to avoid security systems and not set off any alarms. He is prepared for any eventuality, but he plans for his mission to run as smoothly as possible. "Get in and get out" is his motto.

few things that might help you conquer this style of spying:

NING – For this mission, it's always good to know the land-
ahead of time. So scout ahead, or make sure you have a map.

ARATION – If this is a night mission, bring a flashlight. If
s a guard dog, bring doggy treats. Always be ready for any-

– Yeah, this is a hard one for everyone (especially me!), but
portant. Sometimes, it's better to wait than to rush in.

NUITY – Be careful to leave everything as you found it
s your mission states otherwise)! That means, don't break
ng. And if you move something, make sure you put it back
y as you found it, or at least give the impression that you
e whole point of being stealthy is that no one will
t you were there!

> To practice this method, give yourself
> a low-key mission—like sneaking into
> the kitchen in the middle of the night.
> Wait until your parents go to bed, then
> very quietly sneak into the kitchen,
> and do something subtle like move a
> box of cereal from the pantry to the
> refrigerator. In the morning, you can
> enjoy watching your mom or dad look
> for their favorite cereal and they'll
> never know you were the one who
> moved it. It's all about being sneaky,
> after all!

? DRESS TO IMPRESS

NEVER UNDERESTIMATE THE POWER OF A *GOOD WIG.*

No matter what kind of spying you plan to do, you'll need to dress the part. If you're sneaking into your sister's room to plant fake insects in her bed, you'll probably want to wear all black so you blend into the shadows. If you're attending a party to get someone to tell you about a secret, you should wear clothes that are appropriate for the occasion. And if you're going undercover at a clown academy, well, you're going to want to break out that white face paint, a red wig, and some big, funny clown shoes.

Another method of spying is disguising yourself to fit into any situation. Some government agents use skin paint and **"prosthetics"** (a fancy way of saying artificial body parts) to make themselves look like someone they're not. You can use anything to do this . . . masks, makeup, wigs, body suits, clothes, you name it.

Maybe you want to eavesdrop on someone at the park, but you don't want them to recognize you. How do you do that? Change your appearance! Here're a few ways to make you look like someone else:

- Stuff a pillow in your shirt and/or pants to add to the illusion of being bigger than you are.

- Wear a wig! The more different the hair color and style, the less likely people will think it's you. If the wig isn't enough, add a hat!

- Add glasses or even better—sunglasses! The bigger and darker the pair of sunglasses, the better.

- Draw on your face. Add freckles, or a giant mole, or maybe just a bunch of pimples.

- Change your clothes. If you usually wear jeans and a T-shirt, try something a little fancier, like a button-down shirt and a tie. Or maybe borrow some clothes from your grandpa. Then no one will recognize you.

SPY SOCIETY!

History has proven that some of the best spies are women. Intelligent and cunning, the four women highlighted here have served as everything from guides and couriers to analysts and top-notch spies. You may not have heard all of their names, but that's the way good spies like it. Their heroic activities are supposed to be secretive, and even though they often don't get credit for their work, they never let that stop them from completing important missions.

Margaretha Geertruida Zelle MacLeod—better known as Mata Hari—was a Dutch dancer who was convicted of being a spy in France under charges of working for Germany during World War I.

Well-known as a talented singer and actress, St. Louis's Josephine Baker was so famous that during World War II, the Nazis allowed her passage without checking her sheet music— which hid French resistance secrets written in invisible ink!

After joining Britain's Special Ops, Nancy Wake established a spy network so successful that she became one of the German secret police's biggest targets. Nicknamed the "White Mouse," she became infamous after killing a sentry with her bare hands.

Harriet Tubman is well-known for her life as a "conductor" in the Underground Railroad, which led hundreds of escaped slaves to freedom, but she was also a spy for the Union during the Civil War, helping save an untold number of lives.

BODY LANGUAGE AND SPOKEN LANGUAGE

A *GOOD* SPY USES *BOTH*.

Dressing the part is only half the battle. You have to remember that body language is just as important as your disguise if you want to be believable. Body language is an unspoken communication, wherein a person may reveal clues about themselves or their true feelings through actions, movements, or facial expressions. The same goes for speaking. If you use your normal voice when you're supposed to be someone else, you're going to get caught. A good spy is like an actor—always ready to take on an entirely new role as a different person!

For example, if you need to go
undercover as an old man, then research the role.
Watch your own grandpa, or watch some grandpas on
TV. You can dress like an old man easily, but do you act
and sound like one? Add a cane, and use it as if you have a limp.
Walk slower. Mutter under your breath.

If you need to go undercover as a foreign exchange student, then
make sure to practice the accent ahead of time. The best way to do
that is to watch an actor with the same accent, or maybe even watch
foreign films or shows. Whether it's British, Australian, French, or
Russian, practice, practice, practice!

And if you need to go undercover as a shark, well, I guess
make sure you learn how to swim, hold your breath
for long periods of time, and eat
raw fish (gross).

OKAY, SO IF YOU HAVEN'T FIGURED IT OUT, SPIES NEED TO LIE . . . A LOT.

I'm not saying you should lie to your mom and dad, but in the spy biz, it's good to be able to tell a believable lie and get away with it. But there's something even more important than being able to tell a lie—being able to tell if someone else is lying!

There are a few good ways to do this, and I've put together the best of the best. After all, lying makes most people feel guilty and uncomfortable, which in turn makes the body react in certain ways. If you can learn to read these clues, you'll be a living lie detector machine. Lots of people use these techniques. Police use them in interrogations, lawyers and judges use them in the courtroom, and teachers use them to find out if a dog did or didn't eat your homework.

So read these, and memorize them.
That way, no one can fool you. Or can they?

1.) Detecting lies in the face and eyes

There's an old saying that goes, "The eyes are the windows to the soul." And in this instance, it's true! If you're asking someone questions and they cannot maintain eye contact, they might be lying. They might look around or their true emotions might bubble to the surface. Sometimes liars can't help themselves from revealing what they're really feeling. So watch their facial expressions and their eyes. But you can't 100 percent trust just this test. Some people are naturally nervous, especially when being questioned. It's a good idea to go through all the following techniques and look at the overall picture.

2.) Detecting lies in body language and nervous tics

The number one giveaway is sweating. People tend to sweat more when they lie, since the body naturally enjoys the truth. Another "tell" when people get nervous is that they fidget, meaning they get restless and antsy, and they start moving. Maybe they're rubbing their arms or scratching their legs more than usual. Or perhaps they can't sit still. Another giveaway is if they start swallowing a lot. When people get nervous, their throat gets dry (probably because they're sweating so much). Make sure to look for nose and mouth touching. Sometimes when people lie, they instinctively put a hand over their mouths, as if they can hide the truth that way.

3.) Pay attention to voices and words

As I previously mentioned, the body doesn't want to lie, so it reveals the truth accidentally if you watch it. Sometimes when people lie, their voice cracks. Sometimes they stutter (especially when making up stories and they aren't sure what to say next), or slur. Sometimes they'll talk really low, or really high. And sometimes, they just start speaking really, really quickly. Other signs of lying include repeating the same words or phrases, giving too many details (as if their story was rehearsed), or changing the subject suddenly. Pay attention to everything and you should be able to figure out what's not true.

4.) Take note of the "big picture"

Sometimes when we really want someone to be guilty, we start to change the facts in our head so that we can convince ourselves of their guilt. It's always good to be as objective as possible when trying to figure out if someone is lying. Some people are easily intimidated, so if you start asking questions, they'll get nervous and shut down. This doesn't mean they're guilty, it just means they get scared easily. So make certain to give your "liar" the benefit of the doubt—unless they have a mustache. Mustaches are a clear sign of liars. If you still aren't sure, ask them to repeat their story. Then, if anything changes, take note. The truth always stands firm, but lies quickly fall apart.

5.) Trust your instincts!

But beyond all of these rules, make sure to include your best weapon—your own gut instinct. It's not easy to trust others, but trusting yourself always comes in handy.

CIPHERS AND SECRET CODES

DECIPHER THE *CIPHER.*

Thousands of years ago in Greece, one official needed to get a secret message to another. Traditional means wouldn't work, so instead of writing a letter, he had the message tattooed on a slave's shaved head. After the slave grew his hair out, the official sent him hundreds of miles to deliver the message. Once he was there, his head was shaved and the message was revealed. This just goes to show the trouble people will go through to hide their meanings. Me? I'm not going to shave your head, and I'm certainly not going to tell you to give anyone a tattoo. There are easier ways . . .

And this is one of my favorite parts of being a spy—creating messages that no one can figure out. If you speak or read and write in a foreign language, you're already doing better than most people. If you know two languages, then you're practically a spy as is. And if you know three or more languages? Well, then you're definitely smarter than me. Maybe you should be writing this book!

Using a cipher (a cool way of saying "secret code") isn't new. Lots of people have used ciphers throughout history, from militaries to governments. These days, some people go to college just to study this stuff. These experts work in the field of cryptography—the practice and study of techniques for secure communication when trying to hide the real meaning from a third party. And by "third party," I mean "the bad guys."

Here are a few ciphers every great spy should know.

CIPHER #1 – MIRROR MESSAGES

Can you write backward? Have you ever tried? If you can, or if you can teach yourself to, this is an easy one. Write out your message, but make each letter backward. Then, to read it, hold your message up to a mirror. If your handwriting isn't too sloppy, you'll be able to read your note in the mirror.

See the alphabet below for help:

ƧYXWVUTƧЯQPONM⅃ꓘJIHGꟻƎDꓷƆBA

Example:

CODE: Ƨ'TƎ⅃ TƎƎM ЯƎTꟻA ⅃OOHƆƧ ЯOꟻ ƎƆI MAƎЯƆ

MESSAGE: LET'S MEET AFTER SCHOOL FOR ICE CREAM.

CIPHER #2 – SPELL IT BACKWARD

If you don't have access to a mirror, or want to be a little trickier, a similar way to create a cipher is to just spell everything backward by rearranging the letters of each word in the opposite order. When people read it, it'll look like nonsense!

<u>Example:</u>

CODE: **OD UOY WONK OHW DETRAF GNIRUD EHT YROTSIH NOSSEL?**

MESSAGE: DO YOU KNOW WHO FARTED DURING THE HISTORY LESSON?

CIPHER #3 – REVERSE ALPHABET

So for this one, you'll need to make a key, or a way to translate the code. It's pretty easy, though. You take the alphabet and write it out from A to Z on your paper. Just beneath it, write the alphabet again, but go backward.

Key:

A B C D E F G H I J K L M N O P Q R S T U V W X Y Z
Z Y X W V U T S R Q P O N M L K J I H G F E D C B A

Example:

CODE: **DZMG GL DZGXS Z NLERV GLMRTSG?**

MESSAGE: WANT TO WATCH A MOVIE TONIGHT?

CIPHER #4 – PIGPEN!

For years, I didn't understand this cipher. Then when I found out, I was like, "Oh, that's really easy!" I wish I'd had a spymaster as smart and good-looking as the one you have teaching you!

To create the key for pigpen, draw two grids—the first like a tic-tac-toe board, and the other like a big "X." Then fill in your letters as shown. The first letter in each space is represented by the lines around it. So is the second letter, but it also gets a dot. For example, the letter A looks like a backward L. B looks the same, but with a dot added to it.

Sometimes it helps to practice writing a few words first—that way you get the hang of it before moving on to sentences and longer messages. The cool thing about pigpen is that the message looks like Egyptian hieroglyphics and most people will just think you're being artsy. But really, you're being a spy.

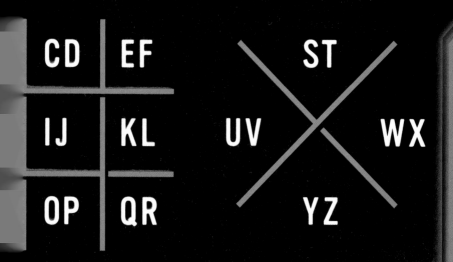

CD | EF   ST

IJ | KL   UV   WX

OP | QR   YZ

CIPHERS ARE COOL

NO ONE UNDERSTANDS

WHAT IM WRITING

GE: **CIPHERS ARE COOL.**
NO ONE UNDERSTANDS
WHAT I'M WRITING!

CIPHER #5 – THE GRID

This is another do-it-yourself secret code. You can follow the grid I've made below, or you can change it up and make your own. Just make sure whatever you do, that you share the key with whomever you need to decipher your message. Otherwise, they're going to look at you like you're crazy. And spies aren't crazy! Well, okay, maybe a little...

*I put "i" and "j" together, but you can just as easily put any other two letters in the same box. Or even better, add a new row with punctuation or smiley faces. Up to you!

Example:

CODE: B4 C5.C1.A1.C3   C4.C3
        D3.C1.A5.A5.C5.B4.C3.B2
        A4.D5.D2.B4.C3.B2   C2.A1.D4.B3
        A3.C1.A1.D3.D3

KEY	1	2	3	4	5
A	a	b	c	d	e
B	f	g	h	i or j	k
C	l	m	n	o	p
D	q	r	s	t	u
E	v	w	x	y	z

MESSAGE: I PLAN ON
         SLEEPING
         DURING MATH
         CLASS.

42

CIPHER #6 – PIG LATIN!

Some spies and soldiers use sign language to communicate on the field of battle, but if you don't have time to do that, you and a friend can teach yourself this fun cipher. You can certainly write this one down too, but it's so much better as a spoken cipher. If you and a friend can learn this one, it'll give you hours of hilarious fun, and it will almost certainly annoy every adult around you!

Pig Latin is an altered language, and though it's popular, it can be hard for some people to figure out.

To convert a word into pig Latin, remove the first consonant, place it at the end of the word, and add the fragment "ay." For instance:

• **DOG BECOMES** og-day.

• **CAKE BECOMES** ake-cay.

• **TEACHER BECOMES** eacher-tay.

For a word beginning with a vowel (a, e, i, o, u), move the first vowel to the end and add the syllable "hay."

• **EAT BECOMES** at-ehay.

• **ORANGE BECOMES** range-ohay.

• **UNIVERSE BECOMES** niverse-uhay.

Pig Latin can be easily understood when spoken at a regular pace, so try to talk faster. Or even better—invent your own language!

Re-ahay ou-yay tarting-say o-tay nderstand-uhay iphers-cay?

Ood-gay or-fay ou-yay!

TRUE SPY STORIES!

SPY ANIMALS?!

You read correctly. From insects to birds, all kinds of animals have been trained and used to spy over the years. As technology continues to develop, this will likely begin to happen more and more often. But for now, let's look back at some recent acts of animal espionage!

In the 1960s, the CIA reportedly explored using cats as spies! The project—dubbed "Acoustic Kitty"—meant to insert microphones and transmitters into the feline agents. The tail was even used as an antenna. Unfortunately, the first wired cat took a few steps toward its target and was run over by a taxi.

Iran claimed to have discovered "spy pigeons" near a nuclear facility in 2008. This would have seemed weird, but there are stories of camera-carrying pigeons dating back to 1903, when a German engineer experimented with the idea. In the past, these birds were used for sending messages. One such pigeon, Cher Ami, won a medal for saving US lives during World War I.

The US Navy has recruited sea lions and dolphins for their Marine Mammal Program. Both animals, known for their intelligence, have been trained to sweep for mines, carry cameras, and even cuff underwater suspects!

You might think insects are too small to be spies, but in the next few years, you could be proven wrong! Technology is so advanced (and so small) that electrodes, batteries, and video cameras can be fitted onto insects, such as moths and beetles.

? TRUST...

So this is really the easiest lesson of the whole book. Are you ready for it?

When you're a spy, do you know whom you can trust?

NOBODY!!!!*

*except yourself—but only if you haven't been kidnapped and brainwashed by mad scientists or killer robots.

Well, I think I've done all I can for you. Study this book backward and forward and upside down, and once you've mastered these skills, you'll be on your way to being a most formidable spy.

What's that? What do you mean you're already a spy? You only pretended to be a trainee to steal my secrets and sell them to the highest bidder?! That is awful and mean, and even kind of smart, and downright diabolical . . .

Well done! It looks like you have what it takes after all. I suppose congratulations are in order, as you're well on your way to becoming the world's next greatest spy!

GLOSSARY

body language: the unspoken communication of actions, movements, or facial expressions

cipher: a secret code

covert: subtle or disguised

cryptography: techniques for secure communication when trying to hide the real meaning of something from a third party

deception: the act of misleading

espionage: the act of spying

handle: a code name

infiltration: to go behind enemy lines

intel: intelligence, information

operative: a secret agent

overt: not hidden or secret

partisan: a supporter of a particular group or cause

prosthetics: artificial body parts

subversion: the act of destroying or undermining something